Experiments with
HEAT

TREVOR COOK

PowerKiDS press.

New York

Published in 2009 by The Rosen Publishing Group, Inc.
29 East 21st Street, New York, NY 10010

Copyright © 2009 Arcturus Publishing Ltd.

Editor: Alex Woolf
Designers: Sally Henry and Trevor Cook
Consultant: Keith Clayson
U.S. Editor: Kara Murray

Picture Credits: Sally Henry and Trevor Cook

Every attempt has been made to clear copyright. Should there be any
inadvertent omission, please apply to the publisher for rectification.

Library of Congress Cataloging-in-Publication Data

Cook, Trevor, 1948–
  Experiments with heat / Trevor Cook.
      p. cm. — (Science lab)
  Includes index.
  ISBN 978-1-4358-2809-4 (library binding) — ISBN 978-1-4358-3222-0 (pbk.)
ISBN 978-1-4042-8027-4 (6-pack)
  1. Heat—Experiments—Juvenile literature. I. Title.
  QC256.C666 2009
  536.078—dc22

                                     2008032713
        5982

Printed in the United States

Contents

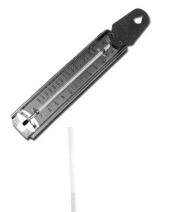

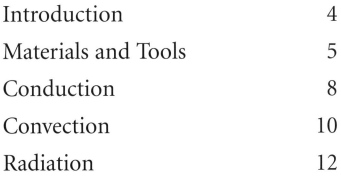

Introduction

Heat is a form of energy. On Earth, most of our heat comes from the Sun, even though it is 92 million miles (148 million km) away.

thermometer

The temperature scale most used in science is *Celsius* (°C). Water boils at 100 °C (212 °F), and *freezes* at 0 °C (32 °F). The lowest possible *temperature* where no heat energy at all remains is –273.15 °C (-459.67 °F), known as absolute zero. It is a point that can't quite be reached, but scientists can get very close to it! We make a *thermometer* on page 20.

The temperature on the surface of the Sun is about 5,500 °C (9,932 °F).

Pompeii worm

All forms of life need heat to live, but not all life-forms need the same amount. In the frozen soils of Alaska and Siberia, there are tiny life-forms called microbes that live and grow in temperatures well below freezing. Meanwhile, under the sea, around deep ocean vents, the Pompeii worm lives and thrives in water at 80 °C (176 °F). How does the walrus deal with freezing sea temperatures? See our experiment on page 16.

Heat energy can move from one place to another in different ways. Look at our experiments on *conduction*, *convection* and *radiation*.

hot-air balloon

radiant heater

heat conductors inside a computer

Some technical or unusual words, shown in *italic* type, are explained in the glossary on page 31.

Materials and Tools

For our experiments, you may have to buy a few things from a store but you should easily find most of what you need around the house.

20 minutes This tells you about how long a project should take.

 This symbol means you might need adult help.

Wire You will need fairly thin, bendable wire. It's usually available in hardware stores. You can also use the kind of garden wire that's used for securing plants.

Glue stick This is mostly used for sticking paper to paper. Rubber cement is a rubbery glue that sticks most things to most other things!

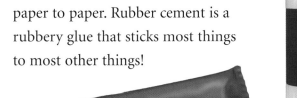

Kettle Ask to use an old kettle if you can – either an electric kettle or one you can heat up on a stove. You will need an adult to help.

Hair dryer Ask before you borrow this and use it with care. It's an instant source of hot air.

Clock You'll need one that shows seconds to help record time in some of the experiments. Put your time records in a notebook to compare results.

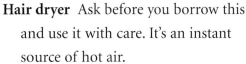

Tape We use tape to hold things in position. Masking tape or clear packing tape will do.

Scissors Ask an adult for a pair of safety scissors that you can use for your experiments.

Tea light Always use with care, and never leave lighted candles unattended. Watch out for hot wax. Follow our instructions exactly.

Oven mitt Always use padded gloves if you are handling anything hot. Avoid painful burns!

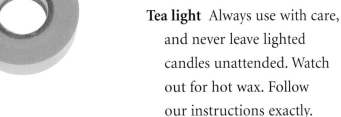 

Tubes Collect cardboard tubes from paper towels or other paper rolls to use in experiments.

Thread Thread is used for sewing. Ask permission to use some.

Thermometer Sometimes these are used in cooking so you may find one in the kitchen.

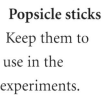

Popsicle sticks Keep them to use in the experiments.

Aluminum foil Aluminum foil, also called tin foil, usually comes on cardboard rolls. Keep any old rolls, we'll need them later.

Matches Try to get extra long matches. Take care!

Mugs You will probably find everyday mugs in the kitchen. Don't use the good china!

Foam cups Keep any foam cups you may find, they will be useful for our experiments.

Cutlery Ask permission before you use knives and forks. There may be some old cutlery you can use.

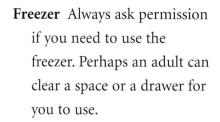

Bubble wrap Bubbles of air are sealed between layers of thin plastic. It's mostly used for packaging, but we use it for insulation.

Freezer Always ask permission if you need to use the freezer. Perhaps an adult can clear a space or a drawer for you to use.

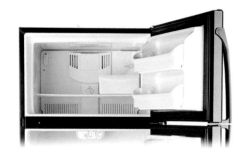

Saucepan Use an old saucepan if possible. You should ask an adult to help you use the stove.

Tissue paper It's often used for wrapping presents or glassware and is available from craft shops in sheets of different colors.

Food coloring Small bottles of food coloring, or dyes, are available from supermarkets for coloring cakes and other sweets. It's very strong. You will only need a few drops.

Plasticine If you don't already have some of this popular modeling material, you can get it from a good craft shop.

Friends can help Do the experiments with your friends!

Salt You'll need a lot of salt for your experiments!

Ice cubes Collect some ice cubes from your freezer tray, put them in a plastic bag then back into the freezer, ready for use in experiments.

Straws We'll need some drinking straws. Try the kitchen drawer!

Plastic bottles Ask an adult for empty plastic bottles. The ones used for water and soda are best.

Sandwich bags You'll need some plastic sandwich bags for your margarine experiment!

Shoe box Every time someone has new shoes, there might be a box available. Save them for experiments.

Cardboard Cut thin cardboard from old cereal boxes so you don't have to buy sheets from the art shop!

Conduction

25 minutes

Conduction is the way heat is carried through solid materials, for example, from a kitchen stove through the saucepan to the food.

You will need:

- hot water (kettle)
- mug
- long, thin objects made of different materials, such as:
  forks and spoons
  wire coat hanger
  plastic straw
  knitting needles
- clock that shows seconds

The plan

We are going to find out which materials are best at conducting heat.

What to do:

1 Heat some water in a kettle.

2 Put some hot water in the mug. Be careful!

8

3 Place the first object in the water. Hold the other end. See how long it takes to become too hot to hold.

4 Fill the mug with hot water again and try other things. This time we're testing a metal coat hanger.

5 Now try a plastic drinking straw.

6 This is a wooden spoon.

What's going on?

Energy in the form of heat passes from one molecule to the next along the object. Metals conduct heat well and so are called good conductors. Nonmetals, like plastics and wood, are not good conductors and are called *insulators*.

What else can you do?

Try comparing results for objects made of the same material, but of different thicknesses.

Jargon Buster
A **molecule** is the smallest unit of a compound.

Convection

The way that heat is carried through liquids and gases, for example, a radiator heating up a whole room, is called convection.

The plan

We are going to show a convection current in air by using *smoke*.

You will need:

- shoe box with a lid
- two paper towel roll tubes
- tea light in a holder
- one popsicle stick
- tape
- thin cardboard
- thread

What to do:

1 Draw two circles on the lid of the shoe box, one at each end. Draw around the end of the paper towel roll tube.

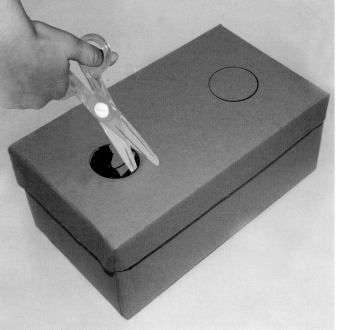

2 Cut the holes out and stick the tubes in place with tape.

3 Light the tea light and put it in the shoe box so that it is under one of the tubes when the lid goes on.

4 Light the popsicle stick with a match. (Ask an adult to help.) Then blow the flame out.

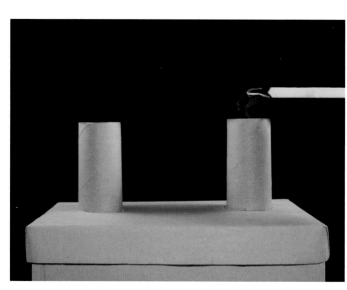

5 Hold the glowing stick over the tube that doesn't have the tea light under it.

What's going on?

The candle flame heats the air, which rises up through the tube. Cooler air is heavier and is drawn down the other tube. Air travels through the box, drawing the smoke with it.

What else can you do?

Copy this *spiral* shape onto thin cardboard and cut it out with scissors. Tie a thread to the middle and hang it up. Put a tea light under it – not closer than 8 inches (200 mm) – and watch the rising air make it spin!

6 Smoke goes down the tube and then comes out of the other.

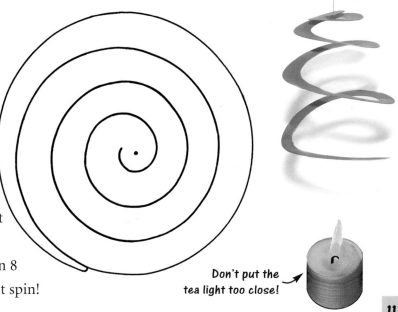

Don't put the tea light too close!

Radiation

Radiation is another way that heat travels through gases. Heat can also travel through a *vacuum* by radiation. An example is the way heat gets to us from the Sun, through space.

The plan

We are going to show how different materials take in heat radiation.

You will need:

- Celsius thermometer
- desk lamp
- different, contrasting materials: for example, things that are light or dark, shiny or dull, cut into pieces of a similar size and shape
- tape

Experiment 1

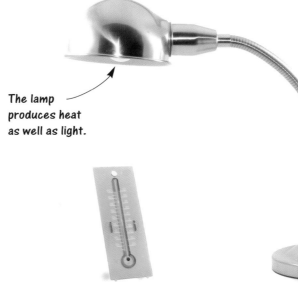

The lamp produces heat as well as light.

1 Find a place to work where the temperature is fairly even. Keep away from direct sunlight and heaters.

2 We are using a desk lamp as a source of radiant heat. Put your thermometer under the lamp.

3 Note the temperature rise after 10 minutes.

What's going on?

Heat is getting to the thermometer by radiation. The heat travels as waves of energy.

Experiment 2

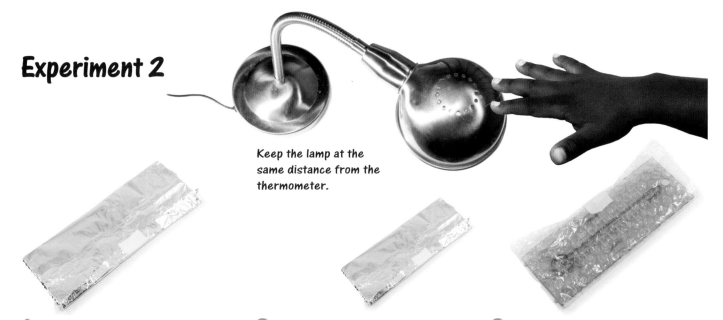

Keep the lamp at the same distance from the thermometer.

1 Start with the thermometer at room temperature again. Wrap it in a fold of test material. Use aluminum foil first. Hold it in place with tape.

2 Put the wrapped thermometer under the lamp. Note the temperature after 10 minutes, then at 10-minute periods.

3 Let the thermometer cool back to room temperature, then repeat with other materials. You can try combinations, too!

4 Make a graph to show your results. It should show that shiny material insulates against radiant heat better than dull material. Lighter material insulates better than darker material.

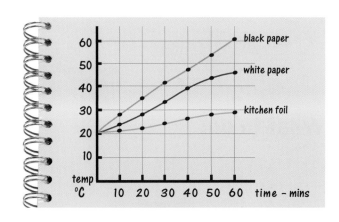

What's going on?

Dark, dull surfaces take in the waves and soak up the heat. Light, shiny surfaces reflect the waves and stay cooler.

What else can you do?

Can radiation pass through solids? Try putting a sheet of cardboard, glass or plastic between the radiator and the thermometer.

Jargon Buster

Radiant heat is heat given off by something hot. **Radiation** is a general word used for energy that travels in waves. **Radiator** describes something that gives off energy. The radiators in our homes give off heat by a mixture of radiation and convection.

Insulation

Insulation is a quality a material has when it does not easily allow heat to pass through it.

The plan

We are going to show how different materials can cut down heat loss.

You will need:

- material to use as insulation, such as bubble wrap, tin foil, cardboard, sheets of plastic (cut from plastic bags), felt, sponges, paper
- at least five foam cups
- a few other cups or mugs – about the same size as the insulated ones
- Celsius thermometer
- pencil and paper
- clock that shows seconds

What to do:

1 Set up at least five foam cups and two made of other materials.

2 Cut disks of different materials to make covers for the cups. Make combinations of materials, too.

paper   bubble   sponge

tin foil   plastic

3 Put the lids on the cups they are to go on. Make a note of which is which on labels.

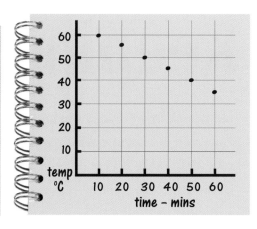

4 Heat up water in a kettle. When it's hot, pour some water into each of the containers.

5 Take the temperature in each cup, then quickly put its cover on.

6 Note the water temperature in each cup on a graph.

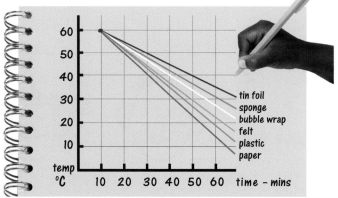

7 Wait for 10 minutes. Take the temperature in each cup again. Stir the water before taking the reading.

8 Plot points on your graph. Repeat at 10 minute intervals. The more times you do this, the better.

What's going on?

With no cover, heat is quickly lost to the air. Layers containing trapped air are better insulators. The best cover combined a layer of aluminum foil, which stopped radiant heat, with a layer of paper towel, which contained air – a bad heat conductor.

What else can you do?

Look around your home to find examples of insulation at work. Look at the different materials in your clothes.

Jargon Buster
Bubble wrap is a plastic sheet with sealed bubbles of air all over it.

Keeping Warm

How does a walrus stay warm?
Have you ever seen a skinny walrus
or a seal that isn't very fat? No? Let's
find out why by making
a *blubber* mitten!

The plan

You're going to find out for yourself how well fat
works as an insulator.

You will need:

- supply of thin plastic sandwich bags
- soft *margarine* at room temperature
- tub
- ice cubes, spoons
- hair elastics, string or wool to put around your wrists
- watch or clock that shows seconds
- assistant

What to do:

1 Scoop margarine into a plastic bag.

2 Put one hand into another plastic bag. Use your left hand if you're right-handed, or your right hand if you're left-handed.

3 Spread a thick layer of margarine over the bag. Now put this hand into the bag that already has margarine in it and squish the margarine around so that it covers your hand. This is your blubber mitten.

4 Ask your friend to fasten the mitten with elastic bands or hair elastics so that they don't slip off, but don't make it too tight. Put two empty plastic bags on the other hand and fasten these, too.

5 Fill the tub with cold water and ice cubes.

6 Put both hands into the ice water. Don't let water into the bags. Use the watch to time how long you can keep each hand in the water before it gets uncomfortable.

What's going on?

The margarine insulates, keeping the warmth of your hand in rather than letting it pass to the water. Animals that live in very cold areas have thick layers of fat under their skin to keep their bodies warm. You feel cold because heat goes from your hand – not because cold comes from the water!

What else can you do?

You could try wearing a wool or padded glove on the hand that doesn't have the blubber mitten. Use a plastic bag to keep it dry. Can you keep the hand in for longer than with just a bag on it? Which is a better insulator, blubber or the fabric glove?

The Water Cycle

Nature has its own water recycling system we call the water *cycle*.

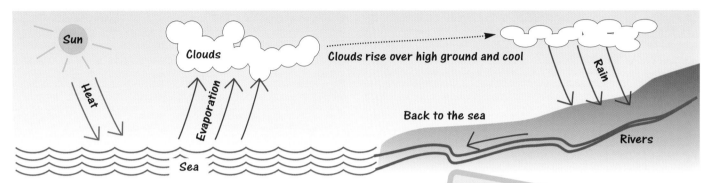

Sun

Heat

Clouds

Evaporation

Clouds rise over high ground and cool

Rain

Back to the sea

Rivers

Sea

The plan

We are going to see how water *evaporates* and condenses.
Then we're going to make our own *clouds*!

You will need:

- kettle
- hand mirror
- oven mitts
- clear, one-liter plastic bottle
- matches
(long ones would be best)

What to do:

1 Fill a kettle half full of water and start heating it.

2 When it begins to boil, turn the kettle off, and use the oven mitts to hold the mirror in the steam.

3 You should soon see water droplets form on the surface of the mirror.

What's going on?

We heated the kettle until the water in it started to change from a liquid (water) to a vapor (steam). The steam is less dense than water and takes up more space, so it pushes its way out of the kettle. Steam touching the surface of the mirror is quickly cooled and changes back to water.

What else can you do?

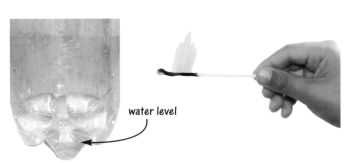

water level

1 Put enough warm water in a bottle to cover the bottom. Light a match and let it burn for a few seconds before blowing it out.

2 Immediately, hold the match in the neck of the bottle to catch as much smoke as you can.

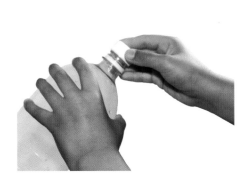

cloud shapes

3 Quickly put the cap on the bottle so as not to lose any smoke.

4 Squeeze the bottle eight or nine times (more may be necessary).

5 When you let the bottle go, you should see little clouds forming inside.

What's going on?

Some of the warm water evaporates inside the bottle. Letting up on the pressure in the bottle cools the air inside so some of the water vapor changes back to liquid droplets. The smoke particles help them to form. Clouds are just collections of water droplets.

Jargon Buster
A **droplet** is a very small drop of liquid. A **particle** is a very small amount of something solid.

Expansion

When things get bigger, they are said to *expand*. Things expand when they are heated and when they are cooled, they contract, or get smaller.

The plan

We are going to make our own thermometer.

You will need:

- plastic bottle
- plastic drinking straw
- plasticine, thermometer
- warm water
- food coloring
- saucepan, stove

This thermometer is made of glass and plastic. It has a special red liquid inside it.

plasticine seal

1 Fill the bottle to the top with cool, colored water.

2 Seal the straw into the neck with plasticine, with most of the straw outside the bottle.

The water has risen from here

to here!

3 Put the bottle in a saucepan of warm water. Heat moves from the water in the pan to the water in the bottle. Water rises up the straw a little.

4 Gently heat the pan. Get an adult to help you with this. As the water in the pan gets hotter, the water rises higher in the straw.

What's going on?

When the water is heated, it expands. The only place it can go is up the straw. The hotter it becomes, the more it expands, so the further up the straw it goes.

What else can you do?

Compare your thermometer with one bought from a store. Make sure it's the kind that can go into very hot water. Use the readings from the other thermometer to label your new thermometer.

Jargon Buster

We **calibrate** a thermometer by comparing it to a standard one and putting the temperature marks in the right places.

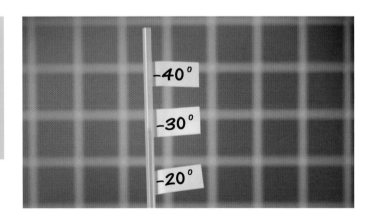

−40°

−30°

−20°

Solid Water

In the last section, we said that most things contract when they cool. Well, when water freezes, it expands!

The plan

We are going to see why it is important not to let your water pipes freeze in the winter.

You will need:

- 2 large plastic bottles
- 1 small plastic bottle
- water
- freezer

Experiment 1

1 Fill the bottle to the top with cold water and fasten the cap.

2 Place it in the freezer and leave it there overnight.

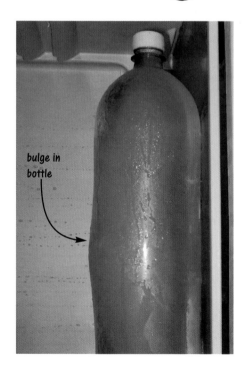

bulge in bottle

3 By the next morning, the bottle will be swollen. It may even have split open!

22

What's going on?

When water freezes, it forms ice crystals, which occupy more space than water molecules. For the same volume, ice is less dense than water. Water is very unusual in this way. Most liquids become more dense as they cool. Water is at its most dense at 4 °C (39 °F).

An *iceberg* is lighter than the water it floats in, so only one-tenth of it is above the water.

Experiment 2

How can we check that one-tenth of floating ice is above the water? Iceberg shapes are very hard to measure!

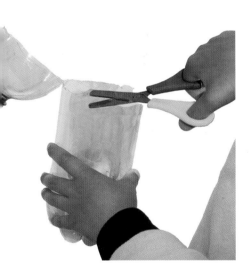

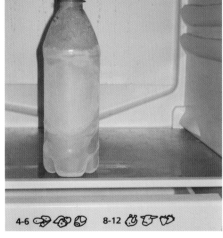

base of ice block

1 Use two plastic bottles, one a little smaller than the other. They need to be fairly straight sided. Cut the top off the larger one. The smaller one should just fit inside it.

2 Fill the smaller one with water but only as far as where it starts to narrow. Place it in the freezer overnight, standing upright.

3 In the morning, get an adult to help you cut the bottle off the ice with scissors. Put some water in the larger bottle and float the ice block in it. You can now measure how much is standing out of the water.

Jargon Buster
Ice and steam are both water but in different **states**.

Antifreeze?

Have you ever wondered why we put salt on the roads when it's icy or snowing?

24 hours

The plan

We are going to see what effect adding salt to water has on the way it freezes.

Experiment 1

plain water

salt solution

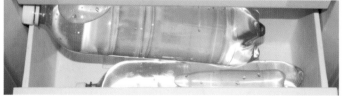

1 Make some salt solution. Add salt to water until no more will *dissolve*.

2 Fill a bottle to the top with salt water and another with the same amount of plain cold water. Put them both in the freezer overnight.

3 In the morning, only the plain water has frozen.

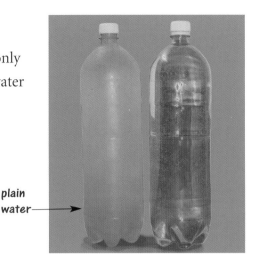

plain water

What's going on?

Impurities in water, in this case salt, lower the freezing point so the water remains liquid.

Experiment 2

Here's a little trick you can try using ice.

1 Put a cube of ice in a glass of plain water.

2 Pour a little salt onto the cube.

3 Hang the end of a piece of thread so that it lies on the salty patch and leave it for a few minutes.

4 After a while, you'll be able to pick up the cube with the thread! Can you figure out what's going on?

Jargon Buster

A **solution** is a mixture of two or more things. Table salt dissolved in water is a solution.

Dissolving

When we put certain things, like salt or sugar, into water, they seem to disappear. In fact, they are still there but have dissolved.

The plan

We are going to see how temperature affects dissolving.

You will need:

- salt
- small saucepan
- two spoons
- thermometer
- water, stove

What to do:

1 Add salt, one spoonful at a time, to a small saucepan of cold water.

2 Use another spoon to stir the water. Count how many spoonfuls can be added before no more will dissolve.

3 Repeat with the water at different temperatures, using the same quantity of water and same size spoon each time.

4 Leave the hottest one to cool.

What's going on?

The hotter the water, the more salt it can hold in solution. When you let the water cool, the salt cannot stay in solution, and it falls out as salt crystals on the bottom of the pan.

What else can you do?

See if the same thing happens with other solids. You could try different kinds of sugar, sand or even chalk dust!

sand

white sugar

crushed chalk

brown sugar

Jargon Buster

When one substance **dissolves** in another, the result is a **solution**.

Hot-Air Balloon

 90 minutes

Here's a demonstration of some of the things we've learned. Getting a balloon off the ground requires a mixture of science and patience!

The plan
We are going to make a balloon powered by hot air.

You will need:

- tissue paper
- cardboard, marker, scissors
- glue stick, paper clips
- about 18 inches (450 mm) of wire
- a hair dryer
- a cardboard or plastic tube (the kind used for mailing posters would work)

What to do:

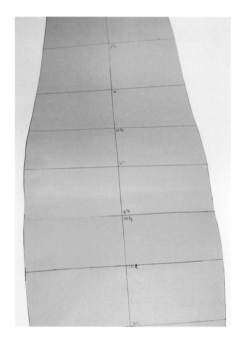

1 Make a copy of the shape shown on page 29 on cardboard. You may have to stick several sheets together. Make your cardboard 48 x 11 inches (1,220 x 280 mm), then draw a center line. Center each measurement on this line. Draw the outline, then cut it out. This is your *template*.

2 The panels of the balloon are eight pieces of tissue paper 48 x 11 inches (1,220 x 280 mm). We had to stick sheets of tissue paper together to make pieces big enough.

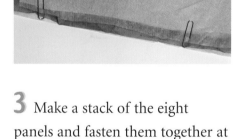

3 Make a stack of the eight panels and fasten them together at the corners with paper clips.

4 Lay the cardboard template on the stack. Carefully draw around the template with a marker.

28

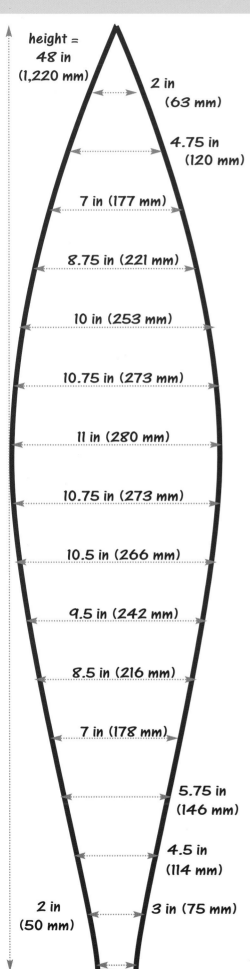

height = 48 in (1,220 mm)

2 in (63 mm)

4.75 in (120 mm)

7 in (177 mm)

8.75 in (221 mm)

10 in (253 mm)

10.75 in (273 mm)

11 in (280 mm)

10.75 in (273 mm)

10.5 in (266 mm)

9.5 in (242 mm)

8.5 in (216 mm)

7 in (178 mm)

5.75 in (146 mm)

4.5 in (114 mm)

2 in (50 mm)

3 in (75 mm)

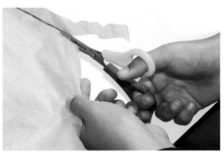

5 Use scissors to cut around your guide line.

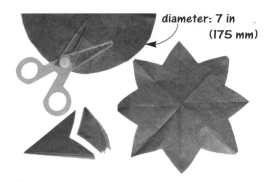

diameter: 7 in (175 mm)

6 Cut a circle from tissue, fold in half twice and cut out the V shape.

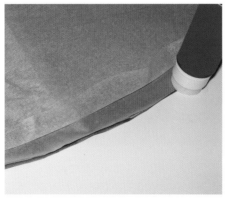

7 Use two panels and lay one on top of the other, but about .3 inch (9 mm) to one side. Put glue on the edge of the lower panel and fold it over the top one.

8 Put on a third piece, moving it .3 inch (9 mm) back in the opposite direction from the last one. Glue it to the lower one.

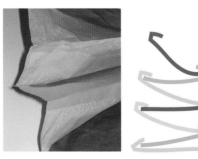

*

9 Continue gluing layers, until you have all eight stuck together. Seen from the end, the stack should look like this*.

10 Check that there are no parts stuck the wrong way. Finish by folding the middle of the stack in and out of the way, then glue and fold the last seam.

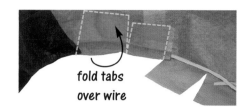

fold tabs
over wire

11 Cut 1-inch-(25 mm) deep tabs in the base of each panel.

12 Make a ring from the wire. Fit it inside the neck of the balloon.

13 Wrap the tabs around the ring and glue.

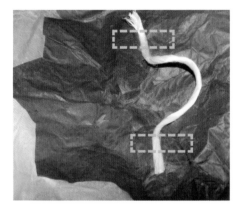

14 Glue the patch on the top. Attach a loop of string with tape.

15 Use a pole to support the balloon.

16 *Inflate* the balloon with the hair dryer and tube. Fix any holes with glue and tissue paper. Finish filling the balloon.

17 Enjoy the flight!

What's going on?

Hot air expands and is lighter than the surrounding air. When the difference is great enough, it can lift itself and the weight of the balloon that contains it.

Glossary

blubber   (BLUH-ber) Fat found on sea mammals, especially whales and seals.

Celsius   (SEL-see-us) The scale of temperature measurement most commonly used in science.

cloud   (KLOWD) A mass of vapor, often water, in air.

conduction   (kun-DUK-shun) Heat moving from a hotter part of a solid to a cooler part.

convection   (kun-VEK-shun) The movement of heat through a liquid or gas caused by hot material rising.

cycle   (SY-kul) A series of events that repeat themselves in the same order.

diameter   (dy-A-meh-ter) The measurement across a circle.

dissolve   (dih-ZOLV) To mix something with a liquid so that they become a solution.

evaporation   (ih-va-puh-RAY-shun) Turning from a liquid to a vapor.

expand   (ek-SPAND) To spread out, or to grow larger.

freeze   (FREEZ) To turn from a liquid to a solid by lowering temperature.

iceberg   (YS-burg) A large mass of ice floating in the sea.

inflate   (in-FLAYT) To fill with a gas, usually air.

insulator   (INT-suh-lay-tur) Something that prevents loss of heat.

margarine   (MAHR-juh-run) Spread used instead of butter, made from vegetable oils and animal fats.

radiation   (ray-dee-AY-shun) A form of heat energy spread by rays or waves. Radiation can travel through a vacuum.

smoke   (SMOHK) Tiny particles, mostly carbon, in the air.

spiral   (SPY-rul) A gradually widening and continuous curve around a central point.

temperature   (TEM-pur-cher) The amount or strength of heat present in something.

template   (TEM-plut) Sometimes called a pattern, a template is a guide for making lots of things the same shape. There is one on page 29 to make the panels for the hot-air balloon.

thermometer   (ther-MAH-meh-ter) A device for measuring temperature.

vacuum   (VA-kyoom) Space that holds absolutely nothing.

Index

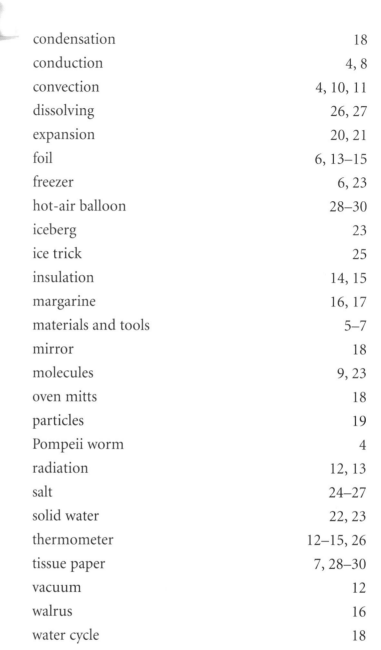

Web Sites

Due to the changing nature of Internet links, PowerKids Press has developed an online list of Web sites related to the subject of this book. This site is updated regularly. Please use this link to access the list:
www.powerkidslinks.com/scilab/heat/